Children and Loss

 caring for yourself and others

Children and Loss

caring for yourself and others

Sue McDermott OBE

redemptorist
p u b l i c a t i o n s

Published by Redemptorist Publications
Alphonsus House, Chawton, Hampshire, GU34 3HQ, UK
Tel: +44 (0)1420 88222, Fax: +44 (0)1420 88805
Email: rp@rpbooks.co.uk, www.rpbooks.co.uk

A registered charity limited by guarantee
Registered in England 3261721

Copyright © Redemptorist Publications 2018
First published June 2018

Series Editor: Sr Janet Fearns
Edited by Caroline Hodgson
Designed by Eliana Thompson

ISBN 978-0-85231-523-1

A CIP catalogue record for this book is available from the British Library.

The publisher gratefully acknowledges permission to use the following copyright material:
Excerpts from the *New Revised Standard Version Bible: Anglicised Edition*, copyright © 1989,
1995, Division of Christian Education of the National Council of the Churches of Christ in
the United States of America. Used by permission. All rights reserved.
Excerpts from *The Jerusalem Bible*, copyright © 1966, Darton, Longman & Todd Ltd. and
Doubleday, a division of Random House, Inc. Reprinted by permission.

Every effort has been made to trace copyright holders and to obtain their permission for the
use of copyright material. The publisher apologises for any errors or omissions and would
be grateful for notification of any corrections that should be incorporated in future reprints
or editions of this book.

Printed by Lithgo Press Ltd.,
Leicester, LE8 6NU

Acknowledgements

The author would like to thank all those children and young people
who have shared the stories, experiences and feelings that are
included in this book, as well as all those facilitators and volunteers
who, through their involvement with Rainbows Bereavement
Support GB, support grieving children and young people.

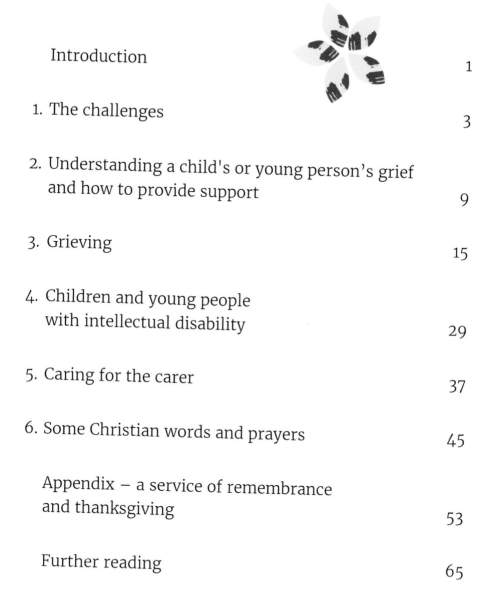

Introduction

The aim of this book is to offer practical help to those offering support in the difficult area of childhood bereavement.

There are no easy answers to what to say or do when faced with a child or young person who has experienced the loss of a significant adult in their lives. But it isn't an option to do nothing or just avoid the difficult situation. Whatever our response it will be significant to the bereaved, and by ignoring the loss we are sending a powerful negative message.

Although this book is primarily concerned with bereavement through death it should also be remembered that other significant losses may occur in a child's or young person's life and they too are bereavements, for example loss due to refugee status, loss of trust due to abuse or neglect, loss due to separation or divorce.

Each bereavement is unique to the individual and each individual's response to bereavement will be different, even within a family. The bereavement belongs to those who have experienced the loss and we can only hope to be compassionate companions on their journey.

There are sections in the book for "those who care" and for "those who suffer" but in many cases this will be the same person. A parent may experience the death of a partner and be suffering, but also be caring for children who have experienced the death of a parent. If we are to "walk with" the bereaved, we may be able to help by giving the adult a little space to grieve themselves, while being assured that their child is receiving support.

Bereavement organisations recognise that the child or young person may well need someone outside of the family to share their feelings. This isn't a criticism of the remaining parent, but it does allow him or her to share difficult emotions without worrying about distressing their remaining parent.

1

The challenges

There are many challenges facing anyone offering support to bereaved children and young people, but the challenges facing the bereaved themselves are much greater and lifelong.

What to say and how and where to offer support

When visiting a family following a bereavement, the children may well be overlooked or their voices unheard. It will be important to listen and try and find out what a child or young person understands about the death. This understanding will depend on many factors, including their age, intellectual ability, and their relationship with the deceased. The relationship will differ from person to person in a family and it may be that the deceased wasn't related by blood but "felt like family".

Children often overhear conversations and, if they don't understand what they have heard, they will make the information "fit" what they do know. "Your dad is at peace now" may be interpreted as "your dad is having a really peaceful afternoon after having experienced a lot of pain". This was how a thirteen-year-old initially responded on hearing of the death of her father.

Case study

Mary (not her real name) came along to a training session for adults wishing to facilitate bereavement support for children. During the training she was able to share the feelings she remembered from twenty years previously when her dad had died. She was aged thirteen. Although she was aware that her father was ill, she wasn't aware just how seriously ill he was and that his death was expected in the very near future. When her mum came downstairs to say that her dad was "at peace" she remembers the relief she felt that he was peacefully sleeping and not in pain. This relief only lasted a few moments and the reality dawned, that her dad had died. Mary spoke powerfully about how she wished someone had told her the seriousness of the situation. She had been "protected" from the pain, but this also meant that she wasn't prepared for the loss, hadn't been able to speak about it or had her questions answered. When a collection was taken at the funeral for a cancer charity, she asked why, and was then told that her dad had suffered from cancer. It took many years for Mary to come to terms with what she felt as an exclusion from the family and she struggled to trust those closest to her.

Mary was an intelligent child from a caring, loving family who had tried to protect her from pain. In reality, she needed to feel included in the family's grieving and to receive the necessary knowledge and support.

Although a faith in a loving and caring God may support the adults, it may be difficult for a child to rationalise this loving God beyond "someone who has taken away" their parent. Euphemisms are never helpful for children as they may cause confusion. To have lost someone implies that we may find them. If someone has "gone to sleep with Jesus" – will they wake up? If he or she has "gone to a better place" – didn't they want to stay with me?

The idea of God as a loving father is difficult for many children who have never experienced a loving father and may well not have experienced having a father in their lives.

Each person will react in their own unique way to any form of bereavement and as adults supporting the grieving child or young person we must carefully listen, notice any physical reactions and be aware of any misunderstandings.

An example of this happened when a group of children were told that their teacher had died. She had been away from school for many months, so the youngest children didn't really know her. They heard people say that she was now "in heaven with Jesus". One child reacted by saying that she was sure Mrs X would now be having a lovely time in heaven with Jesus. Another child didn't want to pray any more or hear about Jesus in case he decided that Jesus wanted his mum to have a lovely time in heaven too.

It is much more helpful to speak clearly when someone has died: "I am sorry to hear that [Name] has died," rather than, "I am sorry to hear that [Name] has passed away." There is no confusion with the first statement. It is important that those supporting a grieving child make it clear that they know what has happened and they are not waiting for the child to tell them. This is very important as a child returns to school, out-of-school activity or to their church community. As adults we have a duty to make the transition as easy as possible and, while respecting the wishes of the child, offering to be there if they want to talk.

Schools have an important role in supporting the bereaved child and there are charities able to help in this role. Having a clear bereavement policy and procedures in place will assist the school greatly at this difficult time. The material in *When Somebody Dies* (Rainbows Bereavement Support GB, www.rainbowsgb.org) will help schools in this task.

It is important to ask the child or young person how they want people to react. Do they want people to talk to them about the death, or do they just need to know that people know about it and "just get on with things", knowing that support is there if they need it.

If the child or young person is returning to a community group, for example Brownies or a church group, choir or a youth group, are all the members prepared for their return? It helps everyone if the other members of the group have been prepared and given help to know what to say. A simple, "I'm sorry for your loss," or "I'm sorry to hear about your gran," will help. The bereaved child needs to be reassured that people do know, they don't have to explain anything, and they don't have to talk about it unless they want to.

Death is a difficult subject to approach with a child, but it is up to the adult to make this as easy as possible. When asked to visit and support a bereaved child we need to tell the truth about what has happened in age-appropriate language. If we are to break the news of a death, then it is important that we have the facts as far as they are known; that we try and find an appropriate room to break the news, not on a corridor, and that we tell the truth about what has happened.

One adult, many years after the death of her parent in a road incident, said:

> I was at school and I knew something was wrong when I was called out of class and my brother was too. The headteacher took us to one side and told us that there had been an accident. She said that my daddy was injured and in hospital but that Mummy's injures were too serious and that she had died. I always remember that we were sitting in the cloakroom and there was a smell of wet clothes. I'm sure she was doing her best in a difficult situation but perhaps a warm room would have been better. She hadn't really thought it through because she didn't then know what to do with us then until relatives came for us. Actually, the police were lovely, and they did help. It is strange what you remember.

When we experience significant loss our memories may be of very insignificant things, for example the smell of wet clothes in the cloakroom, but they are linked to the significant event and by that become significant in themselves. The comment that was made, the look that was given or the feeling of not being included – all take on a deeper significance. They will need to be shared in a safe environment, to allow the child to express what they think they have seen or heard and have any misunderstandings clarified.

As we continue to visit and support the child we need to try and actively listen to what she or he is saying, so that we will begin to see what they are feeling, and to correct any misunderstandings. We may have to answer the same question repeatedly. This reassures the child and helps them to process the huge loss in their lives.

We need to be honest about our own feelings and respectful of theirs. Tears can show how much we care and give the child permission to cry and grieve too, but we must also have some control over our reactions. It isn't helpful if we completely lose control. We need to have thought through the situation and gauge how we might respond and almost practise our reactions and

comments. It is important that we keep focused on the child who has experienced the bereavement and not recount our losses.
We need to show empathy but refrain from saying things such as, "It was just the same for me when...", or, "I know what you are feeling." Each bereavement is unique. Each child is unique and our responses to bereavements will also be unique.

2

Understanding a child's or young person's grief and how to provide support

Grief is a distinct human condition. It encompasses the emotions that are felt as a result of being deprived. An external loss event causes grief, but it is felt inside. Grieving is a process of working through loss and it is not a specific emotion, such as sadness, but rather a wide range of often conflicting emotions, beliefs and actions. When someone grieves, it involves the entire self and that is why grief is so exhausting.

A child or young person will grieve in spasms when there is a significant loss. She or he may not be emotionally mature enough to deal with grief throughout each day, so it will come and go, but this does not diminish how deeply he or she feels. We often explain this as "puddle jumping". He or she will jump in and out of emotions, over a day or within an hour. An example of this is a child who has had the death of the parent explained and is very upset, but within the hour is asking to go out to play. This is normal and doesn't diminish the loss he or she is feeling: it is appropriate behaviour and in some ways also protects him or her from being overwhelmed by grief.

It is also important to realise that children don't always have the vocabulary to explain their feelings. Are they happy or relieved at the death of someone who has been in a great deal of pain? This is where structured age-appropriate support groups can help and allow him or her to discover the emotional language they need.

The two key skills in supporting a bereaved child or young person are active listening and keeping a non-judgmental view of all that is shared by him or her, both vocally and in less obvious ways, for example body language and/or changes in levels of activity and alertness. When we are actively listening we need to "show" that we are listening by making small comments and by giving our full attention to him or her, rather than by looking at our watch or mobile phone. The child must be kept safe and we must "work" in a safe way, having full regard of all safeguarding requirements.[1]

Children's and young people's questions

Children and young people may have many questions when hearing of a death. They may be able to verbalise them, or they may need an understanding adult to create the right atmosphere for the questions to be asked. In general circumstances a parent may almost know what a child is about to ask even before the question is asked, but if they too are grieving this will prove more difficult and clues may be missed.

When supporting a family in these circumstances a safe and trusting situation will need to develop before a child will trust the adults with their questions and believe the answers.

If we encourage a child or young person to ask questions, then we must prepare ourselves for some awkward and challenging ones. We need to listen without judging and answer truthfully. One boy came into a group and said: "I'm happy my gran died last night." This wasn't what the adult expected to hear, but she refrained from making a comment, which enabled the child to explain that Gran had a form of dementia and had been very violent towards his mum. He was happy that Mum was safe now. How we respond will determine whether the child trusts us with their feelings, or decides that we don't want to really hear what they have to say.

A child often has at least three unasked questions when she or he is told about the death of a significant person in their life:

1. Did I cause this?

Even though it may have been initially explained to a child that this death is not their fault, they may still feel guilt and need to be supported to ask questions and express their feelings. If the death was sudden, for example in a road incident, the child will have been in shock when things were explained, and it is likely that he or she will not have taken everything in fully.

2. Who will keep me safe?

Children instinctively know that they cannot take care of themselves. This is a fundamental anxiety for all children, even adolescents. While teenagers seemingly are pulling away from the family, they still want to know that there is a protective haven to return to when life gets too frightening or a problem arises.

3. Is this going to happen to me too?

If this is the first death that the child has experienced it will bring them to the reality that everyone dies. It is important that the child realises that yes, we all will die, but it is very unlikely that they will die soon. It is important to keep listening and talking so that these emotions can be freely discussed. Grandma died at seventy, so will everyone die when they are seventy? If the child experiences the death of a sibling, he or she is likely to ask, "Will I die at the same age and from the same illness?" Clear and honest answers are important.

To support a child through a significant loss in the family it is important to explain to a child that:

- The family is still a family, even after the death of a family member.

- The person who has died will live on in everyone's memory and remain part of the family, but in a different way. This is something that a child may come to over time, but not when they have first experienced the huge loss of a parent or a sibling: they just want that person back with them.

- The child did not cause the death.

- Although as adults we know that a child didn't cause a death, she or he may make wrong connections: "Dad had a heart attack because I was too noisy", or "I didn't notice how ill Mum was."

- A death, even after a lingering illness, is never welcome, but it is the last stage of life for everyone. It is no one's "fault".

- Their practical needs will be met as far as is possible, for example they will be picked up from school, tea will be made, they will still see both sets of grandparents.

One young adult shared her feelings about growing up sharing her birthday with the date of her mum's death:

> I have no knowledge or memory of my mum. I was born the day she died. It was very strange visiting her grave and seeing my birthday. I don't know if it was ever said exactly but I

always knew that in some way I was the cause of her death and all the sadness that people felt. I didn't talk about it because that was too difficult and didn't really speak about it until I was expecting my first child. I do wish I had felt that I could ask questions and that I felt okay about being born! I got there in the end but I'm sure it could have helped me in many ways to have had things explained.

After the death of Georgina's grandmother, she was very worried as to who would collect her from school and make her tea. Georgina lived with her mum and always went from school to her gran's until Mum came home from work. Grandad lived there too, but in her eyes, this was Gran's role. It was lovely to hear from Georgina a few weeks later:

Grandad can cook! He makes my tea, not the same as Gran but it is okay, and he says that he loves picking me up and making tea. He likes having someone to eat with and talk to about Gran. I miss Gran but it's okay and I can help Grandad.

Georgina, aged 9

Endnotes

1. Your local parish or diocese will be able to provide support and supply specific detail about safeguarding.

3

Grieving

Understanding a child's possible feelings of grief

Before we look at how a child may express the feelings of grief it is important to consider the age of a child, as this will have an impact on what they understand by death.

The ages given below are only there as guidelines: children are unique and will have their individual reaction to loss. A child's intellectual and emotional age is also an important factor to consider when supporting him or her.

- 0-3 years – a sense of loss but no real understanding of the permanence of death.

- 3-5 years – no understanding of permanence, easily confused, may feel abandoned.

- 5-9 years – magical/fanciful thinking, may feel responsible for the death.

- 9-12 years – understands the finality of death, fearful of own death and that of others, may try to "get on with life".

- 13-16 years – may have difficulty in accepting and talking about death.

Stages of grief are often referred to when bereavement is discussed (see Elisabeth Kübler-Ross in her book published in 1997, *On Death and Dying*) and they cover many emotions that children and adults experience after a significant loss. They are not linear stages, nor do all experience all the stages. But it is still helpful to explore these possible stages of grieving.

There are many theories and studies around bereavement and loss, but this little book is not an academic study. It is here purely to offer some practical ideas to those wishing to be compassionate companions to the bereaved. It is important is that we acknowledge that all reactions are normal for the individual experiencing them and we are there to support them on their journey, to listen and not judge.

The following reactions and feelings are common, but not everyone will experience all of them and not necessarily in this order.

Denial

Children feel numb, shocked and overwhelmed by their feelings, and may fantasise conversations with the person who is no longer present. They may experience emotional or health problems. They really can't believe that the death has happened and are in denial. We need to be very sensitive when speaking with the child but not give false hope that the person will return.

We may pray with the child and family (if appropriate), but not for the dead person to return.

Anger

Children may feel anger towards anyone who is close to them. They may be angry because the loss has happened to their family and has changed it for ever. They may not be able to name their anger, but it may be shown in their actions to those close to them in their family, school, out-of-school activities, and possibly towards God.

They need to be reassured that their anger is a normal reaction to loss and that people can help them learn to cope with their anger without hurting themselves or other people.

Bargaining

Bargaining may seem very unlikely when the bereavement is through death, but very young children will not actually understand the permanence of death as they have no real understanding of time. They may genuinely believe that Daddy or Mummy will come back if they are good. As children mature they learn that death is final, but they may also worry about the other parent dying, or dying themselves, so they will bargain with God or themselves: "If I work hard in school / don't worry Mum / don't ask too many questions, then death will stay away."

Children will attempt to do anything they can to have their life back the way it used to be and for no one else they love to die.

Depression

Children, like adults usually feel very sad when someone they love dies. This is a very normal reaction to loss and one to be understood and supported by those around them. But occasionally this sadness can lead to depression, when the child will feel that life is out of control and perhaps isn't worth living. If a child or adult is depressed and seems unable to get out of this emotional reaction to loss they will need professional help. They will be unable just to "pull themselves out of it". As we support a bereaved child, we need to be aware and look for signs of depression, for example not being interested in anything around them, not being able to make any decisions and being in a state of almost constant anxiety. She or he may even consider joining the person they love by taking their own life. In cases like this it is vital that the signs are not ignored, and that appropriate professional help is available. They may think "Who am I? Why am I still here?"

Fears

Fear of being alone and feelings of loneliness are very common in anyone who is bereaved, as are irrational fears – of noises, the dark, etc. These may suddenly appear and, again, are normal reactions and need to be listened to and taken seriously. The child should be reassured rather than laughed at or made to feel babyish.

Children may not be coping well themselves and added to this is the fear that the adults around them may crumble under the stress of the loss – and then who will take care of them?

Returning to school after a bereavement is often very difficult for children. They need reassurance that they will not have to tell anyone about the death, because they already know. They also need to know whom they can go to if they want to talk, but that it is equally acceptable not to want to talk, so that school becomes a "grief-free" place.

As an "outsider" to the bereavement it may be that we can help the parent by talking to the school if he or she doesn't feel able to deal with it. Children worry about being rejected or bullied when they return to school and need to know that it is okay to tell someone if this happens. Their childhood security and confidence has been shattered by the death of a significant person in their lives.

Acceptance or adjustment

Hopefully you see that, although bereavement has changed a child's life for ever, after a period of time they will adjust and accept the new situation and begin to move forward. They may begin to plan for their future and will have adjusted to a different way of living – not the same, but fine. They will not have forgotten the person who has died and may want to talk about them in a very matter-of-fact way. The fear of forgetting the person will hopefully have lessened over time, and they can begin to live in the here and now while looking forward without guilt.

How long does this process take? There really isn't an answer. Bereavement is individual, as are grief and mourning. Helping children to remember the person who has died will keep the deceased person part of their lives in a healthy way.

Some ideas may help to keep the memories alive:

- Looking at photos and DVDs of happy times together.
- Keeping a box of memories, such as cards, photos, perfume bottles.
- Keeping some small possession from the person.
- Having a special time when we think and pray for the person who has died and the family.
- Listening to music he or she liked.
- Visiting the cemetery, graveyard or place where ashes are scattered.
- Attending a special service of remembrance.
- Listening to people speak about the person who has died.

There are many different activities like these, but we need to be sure that they are both age – and intellectually appropriate to the child. They may need to change with time, ensuring that any sense of guilt is minimised. It is quite natural, for example, that a child may never want to visit a cemetery, or that their visits become less frequent over time.

Of course a child's memories of the deceased may not be happy, and it is okay for him or her to talk about a time when the deceased parent or sibling was angry. It may be that the child has had a difficult or abusive relationship with the deceased, in which case "memory" activities may not be appropriate and the child will need to be supported and have someone they can begin to trust to share their feelings. Great care must be taken to allow the child to speak about his or her memories when they want to, and slowly begin to leave these painful memories behind, recognising that the abuse wasn't their fault, but that of the perpetrator. If we begin to suspect that abuse may be part of the story, we must seek professional help and refer to the appropriate agencies, such as social care services or the police.

Anticipated loss

In some instances the bereavement is anticipated; it is expected and in some way prepared for. The involvement with a hospice may well have become part of the life of a child when their sibling or parent has a life-limiting illness.

When supporting the bereaved child, it is very important to have knowledge of the work that has already been carried out by the hospice. Some young people will want to stay connected with the hospice, while others may feel that it is the last place they want to be. As we try and support the children and young people it is important to realise that this may well be a long journey with many twists and turns.

Often, adults instinctively try to protect a child or young person from knowledge of the inevitable, which may be in the immediate or long-term future. In such a situation the child or young person generally needs understanding and support far more than protection. In most cases she or he will already have perceived that something is seriously wrong and needs to have their worries and feelings recognised and supported. Most children have, when given support, the ability to deal with such difficult experiences.

To answer questions with false statements, half-truths or silence is counterproductive, as it often confuses, distresses and causes unnecessary anxiety.

While working and supporting children and young people who are experiencing anticipatory grief, the following may be useful:

- Confirm the facts about the sick relative.

- Communicate only the information as appropriate (in line with professional/church procedures and the family's wishes).

- Discover what he or she has been told about the illness.

- Never give false hope.

- Allow him or her to talk freely about the sick person.

- Enable him or her to talk freely about how they are feeling.

- Be honest. If you do not know the answer to a question, say so.

- Be careful not to give any information concerning the illness unless the family has given permission or asked you to do this.

A child who has already had a relatively positive experience of bereavement may anticipate it differently to one who has seen a loved one suffer a very painful death.

A number of factors will influence how a child or young person reacts to anticipated loss. The age of the child and their stage of intellectual development will be significant in their understanding of what is going to happen. (For more about this, see chapter 4, "Children and young people with intellectual disability".)

It is helpful to remember that many children have a very different understanding of time from adults, so the length of an illness will have an impact on their emotional understanding. If they have been told that someone is dying they may genuinely want to know when, as they may understand that it will happen immediately. We need to be aware of this when telling the truth to a child. The illness is terminal, but Mum may live for four or five more years. This can seem like a lifetime to a five-year-old child.

Check with the family what has been explained to the child. In many cases the medical staff will be able to give practical support in explaining the condition. Often this information will need to be given in short "bite-size" facts over time, answering questions as they arise.

As all grief is different, so too are all families. If a family has found it easy to talk about difficult issues in the past and to share their feelings it may be that they will find it a little easier to share how they are coping with this illness and potential death.

If you are visiting and supporting a family before a death, then you too will become part of that support network that will hopefully be there before, at and after the time of the death. Continued support after the death is vitally important. Children need to know that their loved one isn't forgotten and that it is still okay to speak about them.

Special times of remembering will be important. Some of these, such as birthdays and anniversaries, will take place within the family, while the school and church can play an important part in creating times when the child knows that people are remembering their family and the person they have lost.

Faith matters

A child's faith background will influence their understanding of death and in many circumstances will offer hope and comfort. It may be that they are angry with God and anyone who comes representing God, or it may be the complete opposite and he or she derives great comfort and help in prayer and support from their faith and church community (see chapter 6, "Some Christian words and prayers").

It is important that children and young people are given the opportunity to question and discuss statements that they don't understand. For example, an eight-year-old boy who had recently received his First Holy Communion, believed that, "Mum can't die because in church you say that if we eat this bread and drink this wine, you will live for ever." The priest tried to explain what was intended by the words "live for ever", but at the time this just made the boy very angry.

Ongoing support is vital to allow the child to express his or her feelings and hopefully allow them to begin to understand and accept the intended meaning of the words.

Grief before death

Grief before death isn't a substitute for grief later on, and won't necessarily shorten the grieving process. It is sometimes a "missed" grief, and it is a privilege to be able to support a child on this stage of their journey. Grief before death does give opportunities for sharing feelings, asking questions, and allowing children and young people to prepare and plan for changes that will take place after the death.

In each case it is very important that support is offered in a safe manner and that the relevant safeguarding procedures are followed. If the child is also being supported by other agencies, for example a hospice or Macmillan Cancer Support, then it is vitally important that everyone works together with the family. The child may feel overwhelmed by support and just wants to get on with things in their own way. We must listen to the family and to the child or young person – it is their bereavement and we are just companions on their journey.

In this section we have talked about supporting a child through the anticipated death of someone close to them. It could be that we are involved with a family where the anticipated death is that of the child themselves, perhaps a child who has a life-limiting illness. In these circumstances it is vitally important that we know what the child has been told about their illness and what support is already being given. While being honest in our answers to the child's questions, we must follow the wishes of the parents. We can only help in the here and now, not dwelling on what the future holds, but supporting the child and the family on their difficult journey.

What really helps

As we've seen, each child or young person is unique, as is each bereavement, but we do know through research that there are some things that help children to survive loss and go on to live fulfilling lives:

- *They receive accurate information.* Children will know if we are just trying to keep them happy. They have a right to the truth as far as they are able to understand.

- *They are allowed and encouraged to ask questions.* A culture of mutual trust and respect will allow children to ask what they need to know. They may take time to trust someone enough to ask those difficult questions.

- *Their questions are answered honestly.* If we don't know the answer then we must say so. When we know that someone is going to die, it is more appropriate to pray for them to be free from pain and cared for, than for them to "get better".

- *They are allowed to participate in family grieving.* If one member of a family dies a child or young person needs to feel part of the grieving that happens. Their grieving may show itself in different ways to that of the adults, but by sharing the grief there is mutual support – they are given permission to grieve.

- *They have someone to whom they can talk and whom they trust.* Children and young people (and adults) need to trust someone before they are able to share their feelings. This trust will take time to develop. It may be a family member, but sometimes it will be easier to speak to someone a little detached from the situation, such as a teacher, a member of the church bereavement team, or someone in a peer-support group.

Although the age of the child or young person will determine the language used, at all times we need to use clear, unambiguous language and respect him or her by giving honest answers.

Funeral services

Each family will want to say farewell to a loved one in their own way. Plans for the funeral may already be in place and the wishes of the deceased very clearly expressed in a way that can be easily followed.

Children and young people may be asked if they wish to attend the funeral, although they may not actually understand what a funeral is. It will take time and patience to explain what will be involved, how long it will last and what will be expected from them.

If we are asked to explain the funeral to a child, we must first find out what the family believes and what language they have already used. They may need to know, for example, that the coffin will be in the church or crematorium, and that it will then be taken away for burial or cremation. This may need careful explanation, and a young child may need reassurance that it is only the person's remains that are in the coffin, and that their loved one can feel no pain.

Some children will be used to "church" language and can accept that the soul of the deceased is with God, but at a time of shock and great sadness we must accept that this understanding may regress.

One child, having had the funeral and burial explained to her, seemed to understand, but then became very upset because her brother John had been frightened of the dark and of worms. Patient repetition of what had been said many times – that it was just John's remains in the coffin, and that his soul, his spirit, was with God, and that he couldn't feel anything – reassured her a little, and possibly avoided an upsetting outburst at the grave.

Over many years of working with adults who experienced childhood bereavement, it is clear to me that people's resentment of not having been involved in their loved one's funeral often stays with them, even when they begin to understand that their exclusion was intended to protect them from sadness and grief. If possible, children and young people need to be included in the family grieving in an appropriate way.

Case Study

A mother was very worried about her daughter attending her grandma's funeral, as the child would see how upset she (the mother) was, and wanted to protect her from this public grieving. The child, aged ten, was quite angry and asked the school to intervene. After much discussion the child did attend the church service and the "party" afterwards. She did get upset, as did her mum, but they were able to comfort each other, and both acknowledged it was okay to feel as they did. The party allowed the child to share in all the memories and stories of her grandma, and to focus on some very happy memories, keeping Grandma "alive" in her mind.

Children need to be able to change their minds, when it comes to the funeral service.

Case Study

One child felt unable to read the words she had written about her mum. Instead of allowing her to feel that she had let someone down, the service leader read the words and the girl then chose to put them in the grave with her mum's coffin. This had been planned for, "just in case". She hadn't let Mum down, she just did it differently.

It may be that the usual adult will not be able to play a supporting role for children during the service, and it can be a good idea to have someone available for this. If a very young child or baby is to attend, for example, then a familiar adult could be at hand to offer a toy to play with, for a toilet trip, or to be a source of comfort. Just as each child reacts to death in their own individual way, so each will respond to the funeral differently, and the support that they need should be planned accordingly.

Children should not be put under pressure to exactly follow the wishes of the deceased, because if they fail to do so they may live with a feeling of failure.

There are many little things that may be suggested to involve children in the whole preparation and attendance at the funeral. Some may feel comfortable writing letters or drawing pictures to put into the coffin. They may wish to put flowers or significant items on the coffin. Whatever they do or don't do will remain with them for many years, probably for the rest of their lives.

Case Study

The dad of a young family was terminally ill and as he neared the end of his life he very bravely spoke with his children and they discussed what his funeral would be like. There were many tears and lots of laughter too. They decided that Dad would have a cardboard coffin, because as a family they prided themselves on their green credentials. When Dad died the children decorated the coffin as they had planned and, although they were very sad, they did feel that this is what "Dad had wanted", and that they were a very important part of the farewell.

As this book is intended to support families in a Christian tradition it may be supposed that everyone will be familiar with the prayers, readings and hymns that are used in a funeral service, whether it is held in a church or crematorium. But of course this may well not be the case. If the family does not regularly attend church, or some members do while others do not, some people may find decisions about readings and hymns, for example, very difficult. It is important to support all family members in their decisions. Care must be taken that nobody feels excluded from anything that is going to take place. The words of the service should be explained, as well as what they will see in the church and what their involvement may be. All of this should be clearly explained and repeated as many times as necessary.

4

Children and young people with intellectual disability

Talking to any child or young person about death is often felt by adults to be very difficult and even more challenging when the child or young person has additional needs. However, grief is a universal emotion and applies to all human beings regardless of their abilities or disabilities. Each person's reaction will be unique to them.

Children with special educational needs, like all other children, will deal with death in many different ways. Some will bounce back as though nothing has happened and adjust to their new life circumstances well, while others will find it extremely difficult to cope.

For some children with additional needs there is a problem with making wrong connections, for example Mum died in hospital: so if I go to hospital I'll die too. One child asked, "What is my number?" After much discussion it became apparent that on the death of a relative, someone had said, "Well, her number was up." We can only imagine what was going through the child's mind.

When bereavement has occurred, all children need to have their questions answered; be listened to; be given appropriate information; helped to feel safe and have people they trust supporting. Children with special educational needs need to be supported professionally and sensitively according to their developmental ability.

When supporting a child with special educational needs in a pastoral role, it will be helpful to speak with the people who know the child well and can explain their particular needs and suggest appropriate strategies.

As we've seen, it's important that all children and young people are spoken to in straightforward language. When it comes to supporting children with additional needs this is more important than ever, and any terms used need to be clear, consistent and unambiguous, for example the words "death", "dead" and "dying" are more appropriate than "asleep", "gone away" and "lost".

Phrases such as "I'm sorry you've 'lost' your mother" or "she's gone to sleep" or "passed away", while often intended to soften the blow, are only likely to complicate a child's or young person's understanding and, ultimately, his or her ability to adjust to reality. For example, using terms relating to sleep can often lead to difficulties with bedtime routines and fears of going to sleep.

A full understanding of death and its implications depends on understanding that:

- death is universal and everyone dies eventually;
- death is an inevitable part of life;
- death is permanent and irreversible.

Many children and young people with additional needs may never reach this level of understanding but will still experience the full emotions of grief while having great difficulty in expressing or communicating their feelings.

It isn't just our cognitive ability that makes up who we are: we have instincts, we are all spiritual beings, with rich emotional lives and the ability to give and receive love, affection and comfort. We must give every grieving individual the best chance to understand, reflect upon, contemplate and come to terms with their grief. We need to offer appropriate support to minimise confusion and uncertainty that might compound the hurt of bereavement.

Following are some general points that may help when supporting children and young people with additional needs who have experienced a significant loss. They need to be:

- Given information appropriate to their understanding.

- Listened to with sensitivity and empathy.

- Helped to feel safe (often school feels a safe and secure place, or their place of worship).

- Able to speak with people they trust; trust takes time to develop.

- Supported using clear, unambiguous language.

- Given appropriate explanations of words associated with death, such as "funeral", "dead", "coffin", "grave".

- Enabled to develop their own understanding with known specific strategies, for example "I know it's okay to feel sad and when I'm feeling sad I listen to some special music and it helps me feel a bit better."

- Offered time to have repeated questions answered and explanations given until they can be processed and understood.

- Secure in the knowledge of clear boundaries, rules and routines.

- Supported over an extended period and at significant times, for example anniversaries, Christmas, Fathers' Day, Mothers' Day.

- Helped to understand and cope with their "new" emotions and the "new" emotions of others.

- Told about any changes in practical arrangements, for example home-to-school transport, new family routines.

- Encouraged to know that it is okay to be happy and have fun.

- Helped to understand that death is a natural part of life and often not as seen on TV or computer games.

When supporting a child or young person with additional needs it is very important that we are aware of the professionals who are already working with him or her. They will be able to advise the best way to speak with the child, what will help their understanding and whether there are any particular situations that will make the child more anxious.

Adapted from When Somebody Dies *and* SunRise *Rainbows Bereavement Support GB*

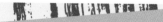

Ongoing support

Families often say that they received wonderful support immediately after a death of a loved one, but once the funeral is over, everyone seems to forget about them.

People rarely forget, but busy lives just take over. Children may appear to have dealt with a bereavement; the tears have stopped and they may have returned to school, but their lives have changed for ever. If they have experienced the death of a close family member, someone who was a regular part of their lives, then their lives will be very different. If they were close to the deceased but didn't see them regularly or often, then they may make themselves believe that they are still alive.

Case Study

A twelve-year-old boy heard of the death of his father who was serving in the armed forces overseas. The family were supported by a family welfare officer. The child attended the funeral and heard wonderful things about the bravery of his father. He was used to Dad being away for a few months at a time and he coped with his grief by allowing himself to believe that Dad was just working away. In some ways this was a good coping strategy that allowed him time to heal, but the rest of the family became worried when they realised that he hadn't taken on board that Dad wasn't ever coming back. They found that a bereavement support group for similar aged children run in his school by Rainbows GB allowed him to share his feelings through a safe and structured programme. In some ways he appeared to regress in his mourning, but he was working through his feelings and finding out that these feelings were okay, and that others had similar feelings too.

There are a number of organisations offering support to bereaved children and young people, including hospices, which often provide support groups and hold memorials for those they've cared for towards the end of their lives. Events may include support meetings and fundraising events. These may be helpful for some children, while others may not want to have anything to do with them, at least not for a while after the death, and that is fine. Even within one family, one child may wish to take part in activities, while another may not. Each individual's wishes should be respected and nobody should be forced to do anything they don't want to.

In a church context there are many traditions for praying for the dead, having a special month when we think of all those who have died and services held on the anniversary of a death. Many families have found an annual remembrance service very helpful. Families are invited to light candles in memory of their loved ones, listen to music and prayers and be as actively involved in the service as they feel able and want to. An example from one church is included at the end of this book.

One family said:

> It was beautiful and sad to remember .... last night. The church looked wonderful in the candlelight. I was so pleased that I brought the children as it helped them to see how much everyone cared about their daddy and about them. They enjoyed the biscuits too!

There are obvious times that may prove difficult. Daddy's birthday, Christmas and the anniversary of a death should all be planned for so that support can be on hand when it's needed. Sometimes it is the more unexpected times that are more difficult to foresee. The barbeque that Daddy always helped at; transferring schools where a sibling is no longer there and many other unforeseen times and triggers.

This is where a trusted adult is very important to a child. The trust is about their feelings as well as about their physical safety. It may be that a child doesn't feel able to share these feelings with their parent, as they don't want to upset them, and when someone not as close to the deceased will be able to help.

As we've said before, it is vital that all safeguarding procedures are followed by anyone in a position of trust. This can be a delicate balance between a child or young person knowing that their confidence will be kept, while at the same time letting the appropriate person or body know if the child is at risk in any way. It is important to be very clear about the regulations and guidelines and seek appropriate support in safeguarding matters. Your local parish or diocese can supply more information.

5

Caring for the carer

When we work closely with bereaved children and young people it can trigger thoughts about our own experiences of loss and dying. It is important to reflect on our own circumstances before we engage in helping children, as we don't want to load our own undealt-with grief on to a child or young person. Sometimes it may even be necessary to take a step back and let others offer support. This may be a difficult decision but an essential one, if our support would place a burden on the child and the family.

If possible anyone working in a ministry that involves bereavement support should have some training which would help them to be aware of their own understanding and personal experience of bereavement. Understanding the grieving process and how it may show itself in different individuals is very helpful and forms part of any bereavement training.

The following questions may give an insight to our own reactions to bereavement. It is important to take a moment to reflect on the questions and remember that there are no right or wrong answers.

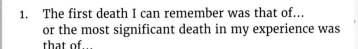

1. The first death I can remember was that of...
    or the most significant death in my experience was
    that of...

2. I was aged...

3. The feelings I had at the time were...

4. Who supported / talked to me at the time?
    How did the support make me feel?

5. The first funeral or other ritual service I attended
    was for... I was aged...

6. The thing I most remember about that
    experience is...

7. When there was a crisis in my family, how was
    it handled?

8. If I have experienced divorce, separation, or other
    loss, how did that make me feel?

9. My own experiences with young people who have
    endured a death, divorce, separation or other loss
    leads me to believe...

10. My way of coping with loss is to...

11. I knew I was ready to "move on" when...

Reflecting on these questions and our answers may give us an insight into our reaction to bereavement and loss as well as an understanding of how others, including children, may respond.

On answering the first question I could clearly remember an aunt dying when I was about seven years old. I remember because I had to stay with friends, but I wasn't really upset as I very rarely saw this relation. Her death really didn't affect my life.

The significant death was much later, just before my nineteenth birthday, when my older sister died very suddenly. This changed where I was studying, my position in the family and I felt a great loneliness having lost my sister and best friend. This significant death has had implications on my life and how I try to support others, particularly children who have experienced bereavement. I was supported by my family, but it wasn't a support that entailed being listened to about my feelings, but rather practical support on how to "move on".

Children need many forms of support when they have experienced a significant loss in their lives. This support many come from many different people. A team of people able to offer support is preferable to relying on one person. This shared ministry both protects those offering support from "burnout" and allows the most appropriate person to offer support to an individual or family. A team will hopefully ensure that the bereavement isn't forgotten and that practical actions are taken, for example sending out invitations for a remembrance evening, checking on how a child is coping in a new school, or making sure that someone says "Hello, how are you doing?" at church.

As we support others we will be of little use if we shut out or hide our own feelings. It is all right for children and families to see us showing our emotions, a few tears are okay, but a total breakdown may create anxiety for a child. If we are to care for others we need to have a support network around us. This may be members of a bereavement team, family members, friends, or other trusted colleagues whom we can tell how we are feeling without breaking the confidentiality of those we are supporting.

Some points to consider:

Use a trusted team to share YOUR emotions. This support is vital for your mental well-being.

Remember that you cannot carry the child's grief for them, but can help them express their grief. We can share their journey just by being there, when trust is established then love and God will be there. Wherever there is love, God is present.

Be careful not to take on too much. Involve others, such as members of a parish or school community. Plan what support you can give. Is it possible to visit every week? Are you able to continue visiting as frequently after the funeral? Particularly when children are involved, it is important to maintain their trust. If you offer too much and then can't fulfil your promise this will damage the trust they have in you. Be realistic and honest. It is better to offer something small and be able to deliver this than offer the proverbial moon and fail to deliver.

Contact other professionals if you are worried about the child's reaction to loss or bereavement – don't carry the worry alone. If you feel anxious that the child may be in danger, either from themselves, such as by self-harming, or from anyone else, then it must be reported to the appropriate person.

To be of help to the child you need to take good care of yourself. Be kind to yourself and remember what you have achieved. The gift you have given may be the time you have spent listening to a child or young person trying to articulate their feelings. You will have given them a safe place to grieve and to start to heal. They can express their feelings without having to worry about placing extra grief on the surviving parent or other siblings.

Bereavement and grieving are exhausting, both for the bereaved and for anyone supporting them. Grieving takes time and there are no time limits. We need to remind ourselves that we can't change what has happened but we can be alongside the child or young person on their journey.

In his book, *Grief in Children*, Atle Dyregrov emphasises self-care. He stresses that, just as children may need permission to be happy and enjoy activities while not forgetting the deceased, so too we need to give ourselves permission to relax and refresh ourselves to allow us to continue in our supporting role.

Prayer journals for children and adults

Prayer journalling is recognised in many Christian traditions as a special way of discovering God in everyday life and of particular help at challenging times. Many schools allocate a weekly time for children to use their own prayer journal.

Bereavement support charities also use journals to give children and young people a special place to record their feelings, draw, add photographs or just doodle. Journalling is like a diary but also very different. It isn't there to record events, but to have as a friend with whom we can share all our emotions without comment or judgement.

For children, a journal allows them to say anything or nothing, to be happy one day and down another; it is part of their journey with all the twists and turns that life involves.

There are journals that are part of a structured bereavement programme for children of all ages (Rainbows Bereavement Support GB) and these take the children through a journey from their unique self and loss, to reaching out to others as they begin to see that life after bereavement will be different, but can be happy and fulfilling. A simple notebook may form a journal, and prompts and comments are often helpful for those times when a child finds it difficult to express their feelings. Some will find drawing much more relaxing than having to think of words, while others will like to add photos or other objects that remind them of happy times with the deceased.

There is no right or wrong way to complete a journal, it will be as individual as the bereavement and the child. Children do have the right to privacy with the comments recorded in their journals.

One child said:

> I can write anything without worrying if I am upsetting my mum and dad. I know they miss ...., but sometimes I am so angry with them because they forget about me.

This was how the child was feeling at the time. He didn't need to be told that Mum and Dad hadn't actually forgotten about him – he just knew how he was feeling at that moment in time.

When supporting a child or young person and possibly the family through a bereavement, having your own personal prayer journal may be a good idea for you, too. It will allow you to reflect on how you are feeling on the journey of support and caring.

Conclusion

Finally, I do hope that you have found some of these suggestions and thoughts helpful. Supporting bereaved children and young people is a great privilege and has a lifelong impact on both the bereaved and on anyone who offers support. The kind word you offer, the time you spend listening, the empathy you show, will all make a positive difference in their lives.
If we can be compassionate companions on part of their journey we may help them to fulfil their true potential as caring and empathetic, well-adjusted adults.

May my voice speak the
words they need to hear,

And be able to offer
the support that brings
consolation and hope.

God, I shall try to be your
ears for listening, your heart
for loving,

Through these times of
sadness and fear,
strengthen my resolve, so that
I may be strong and able to
give the children all they need.

Suzy Yehl Marta
Healing the Hurt,
Restoring the Hope

6

Some Christian words and prayers

Prayers for use with a community, school or parish

Heavenly Father, we are stunned and shocked at the death of [*Name*] and as a community we have gathered together to share our sorrow, our bewilderment, and our pain.

We are all asking the question "Why?", but there seems to be no easy answer.

We pray especially today for *her/his* friends, *her/his* classmates, *her/his* teachers and all who knew *her/him*.

We remember [*Name*] for .... [*List some characteristics or traits of the deceased*].

We just don't understand this Lord, but help us to let go of any anger or any desire for revenge.

May our tears be replaced by smiles when we think of [*Name*], giving thanks for *her/his* life and all that *she/he* was to us and our school/parish/community.

Help us now pick up the pieces once again and to carry on in life as we believe [*Name*] would wish us to.

Adapted from When Somebody Dies, *Rainbows Bereavement Support GB*

Almighty God, you know that it will be very difficult for us at our school / parish without [*Name*].

Bring us the strength and the hope we need to carry on as [*Name*] would have wished us to do.

We thank you Lord, for the special gifts that [*Name*] brought to the [*school / parish*] and shared with us.

May the church and the wider community give thanks for the contribution [*Name*] made to the life of [*place*] and may we redouble our efforts to serve each other, in honour of *her/his* memory.

We ask this through Jesus Christ our Lord.

Amen.

We hold before God all those who are sad because someone they love has died.

We hold before God all those who are sad because someone they know has died.

We hold before God each one of us that we may support each other in the days to come.

We hold before God [*Name*] who has died.
May *she/he* rest in peace.

Amen.

Lord, we look up to you and receive from you,
your blessing,
your strength,
your most holy love.
In the darkest moments of our lives,
let us remember that you are the light,
you are the hope,
you are the courage we need.
Amen.

Lord God, help us find comfort in our sadness,
certainty in our doubt
and the courage to live.
Make our faith strong
Through Christ our Lord.
Amen.

Circle us, Lord.
Keep hope within.
Keep fear without.
Circle us, Lord.
Keep peace within.
Keep darkness out.
Circle us, Lord.
Keep calm within.
Keep turmoil out.
Circle us, Lord.
Keep love within.
Keep anger away.

Private prayers for those providing support or care

Dear God,

Help me as I try and explain death and resurrection to [Name].

Reassure me about the ability of children to understand and their capacity to believe, and make my faith equal to theirs.

Then grant me the right words at the right time to satisfy the mind and comfort the spirit of this your child.

Amen.

Doris Stickney
Water Bugs and Dragonflies

Beatitudes for those that comfort

Blessed are those who hear with their hearts, for they have the gift of empathy.

Blessed are those who in spite of being uncomfortable step forward to comfort the grieving, for their presence shows inner strength.

Blessed are those who refrain from giving advice or platitudes, for their wisdom reminds the bereaved that there are no answers to loss.

Blessed are those who continue to call, visit and send notes long after others have stopped, for they are living examples of compassion.

Blessed are those who understand the timetable of grief and the fragility of bereavement, for they possess a gentle and loving heart.

Suzy Yehl Marta
Healing the Hurt, Restoring the Hope

Footprints in the sand

One night a man had a dream.
He dreamed he was walking along the beach with the Lord.
Across the sky flashed scenes from his life.
For each scene, he noticed two sets of footprints in the sand:
one belonging to him, and the other to the Lord.

When the last scene of his life flashed before him
he looked back, at the footprints in the sand.
He noticed that many times along the path of his life
there was only one set of footprints.
He also noticed that it happened at the very lowest and saddest times of his life.

This really bothered him and he questioned the Lord about it:
"Lord, you said that once I decided to follow you,
you'd walk with me all the way.
But I have noticed that during the most troublesome times in my life
there is only one set of footprints.
I don't understand why when I needed you most you would leave me."

The Lord replied:
"My son, my precious child, I love you and I would never leave you.
During your times of trial and suffering,
when you see only one set of footprints,
it was then that I carried you."

Author unknown
(Several people claim to have
written this poem)

Prayers for children

Children need to be encouraged to pray in any way and with any words they feel comfortable with, but sometimes it is helpful to give some suggestions:

Dear God, I have so many different feelings, some happy and some sad.
Help me to share those feelings with the people I trust.

Dear God, things are difficult for me.
Sometimes it just hurts thinking about it.
Please help me.

Dear God, help me to adjust to the most difficult changes in my life and help me to be open to those who are trying to help me.
Give me the strength to cope with my fear and pain.

Dear God, help me to see your presence in my life and know that you will always be there.

Dear God, sometimes I hurt so much that I want to lash out and hurt others.
Help me to share my feelings with others and find a way to deal with my anger.

Tell Jesus your thoughts and memories of [*Name*]. Let him know your worries and fears.

The Our Father

Our Father, who art in heaven, hallowed be thy name.

Thy kingdom come; thy will be done on earth as it is in heaven.

Give us this day our daily bread and forgive us our trespasses as we forgive those who trespass against us.

And lead us not into temptation but deliver us from evil. For thine is the kingdom, the power and the glory for ever and ever.

Amen.

Eternal rest grant unto [Name] O Lord and let perpetual light shine upon her/him. May she/he rest in peace.

Amen.

Many children will know some prayers from school and may feel comfortable praying these. It may be that a child doesn't want to say anything but is happy to have a quiet time with music and a candle. If children are used to saying prayers at bedtime this will probably be the time they wish to remember and mention the deceased.

Appendix – a service of remembrance and thanksgiving

This service was devised and created by members of the congregation of Our Lady of the Assumption Catholic Parish in Stainforth, Doncaster, South Yorkshire, where it is held each November. A general invitation is sent out to all parishioners, and individual invitations are sent to the families of those whose funeral services have been held in the church in the previous twelve months, regardless of whether they usually attend church.

This service is offered to any community to be used and adapted according to their own particular needs.

You might find the following helpful in your preparation:

- your parish remembrance book
- the register of those who have died
- candles
- blessed water
- an Easter candle
- a remembrance tree (this might be a painted branch, and should be large enough to hang notes from)
- a symbol of thanksgiving for the life of anyone being remembered (you could invite friends and family members in advance to bring something to the service).

- the music and words of hymns. In this case the following are suggested, although you might prefer others:
  - "A Time to Remember", by Liam Lawton
  - "Be Still for the Presence of the Lord, the Holy One is Here", by David J. Evans
  - Stuart Townend's arrangement of Psalm 23: "The Lord's My Shepherd, I'll Not Want"
  - "Do Not be Afraid, for I Have Redeemed You", by Gerard Markland
  - "I Will Come to You in the Silence", by David Haas

A parish service of remembrance and thanksgiving

The music playing before we begin is "A Time to Remember" by Liam Lawton.

Leader:
To each and every person here, thank you for coming, you are most warmly welcome.

Words of welcome and introduction

Litany of welcome

Leader:

For all who have lost someone they love, welcome.
You, who have lost your husband, welcome.
You, who have lost your wife, welcome.
You, who have lost your partner, welcome.
You, who have lost your father, welcome.
You, who have lost your mother, welcome.
You, who have lost your son, welcome.
You, who have lost your daughter, welcome.
You, who have lost your grandfather, welcome.
You, who have lost your grandmother, welcome.
You, who have lost your sister, welcome.
You, who have lost your brother, welcome.
You, who have lost your friend, welcome.
You, who have lost hope, welcome.
You, who have faith, welcome.
You, who find religious faith difficult, welcome.

In silence, we now gather our symbols of birth, life, death, resurrection, hope and thanksgiving. We bring forward our parish remembrance book and our register of those who have died as we remember our own loved ones who have gone before us. We light the rainbow candles, symbol of human hope; we pour blessed water into our baptismal font, symbol of our life in Christ; we light our Easter candle, symbol of the new dawn of Easter, of everlasting life, of resurrection, and we bring forward a symbol of thanksgiving for the lives of all those whom we have loved. We entrust them all to our God.

Please join us as we sing our first hymn.

All sing:

"Be Still for the Presence of the Lord, the Holy One is Here",
by David J. Evans.

Leader:

Creator God, we thank you for everlasting life, for life that knows no end, for the joys and blessings of the new life our loved ones now experience and for bringing us love and hope through the life, death and resurrection of your son Jesus. Amen.

Reading and reflection

Reader:

A reading from the Gospel according to St John 14:1–3. My brothers and sisters, Jesus says:

Do not let your hearts be troubled. Trust in God still, and trust in me. There are many rooms in my Father's house; if there were not, I should have told you... and after I have gone and prepared you a place, I shall return to take you with me; so that where I am you may be too.

The Gospel of the Lord.

All say together:

Praise to you, Lord Jesus Christ.

Leader:

Please join us as we sing our second hymn.

All sing:

Stuart Townend's arrangement of Psalm 23: "The Lord's My Shepherd, I'll Not Want".

The reflection

Leader:

Death will come to us all sometime, but when we lose someone we love, we react in many different ways at different times...

Sometimes, we might feel relieved:

> Because we know they won't suffer any more.
> Because their burden has been taken away.
> Because they are at peace.

Sometimes we may feel guilt:

> Because we feel relieved.
> Because we were at breaking point.
> Because we couldn't cope much longer.

Sometimes we may feel frightened:

> Because they went so suddenly.
> Because we weren't ready for their death.
> Because they have left us to cope alone.
> Because we still need them.

Sometimes we may feel angry:

> Because they were so much in pain.
> Because they were too young.
> Because God should not have let this happen.

Sometimes we feel so sad:

> Because they meant so much to us.
> Because they were loved so much.
> Because we miss them so much.

But in all of these mixed emotions of grief and thankfulness for those we have loved, we are able to have hope and trust and peace; for Jesus says to us "I am the resurrection and the life".

The reading of the names and lighting of candles

Leader:

It is in that spirit of hope and trust that we now name all those who have died in this community and had funeral services here since [*Month of last remembrance service*].

We also name those whom people here tonight have asked us to remember.

We read out names and then while we sing our hymn, please (slowly and carefully) come forward and light a candle as a personal act of remembrance, love and thanksgiving.

You may also wish to remember a loved one by hanging their name on our tree which will remain in place for [*X days/weeks*].

Please join us as we sing our next hymn.

All sing:

"Do Not be Afraid, for I Have Redeemed You",
by Gerard Markland

A time of silence

Prayers of petition

Leader:

Heavenly Father, conscious of your presence with us now, we ask you to listen to our prayers.

Leader or prayer leader:

We pray for all the people named tonight whom we have loved and who have died. Help us to hand them over to your loving care. Lord, hear us.

All: Lord, graciously hear us.

Leader or prayer leader:

Lord, you see us when we are sad and lonely, or when we feel angry or betrayed. Strengthen our faith; help us to accept the death of those we have loved, help us to be thankful for their lives and give us peace of heart. Lord, hear us.

All: Lord, graciously hear us.

Leader or prayer leader:

Lord, we thank you for the support of family and friends. Bless them for their goodness and understanding. Lord, hear us.

All: Lord, graciously hear us.

Leader or prayer leader:

Lord, we thank you for the person of Mary, the mother of Jesus, who knew the pain of loss as well as the joy of resurrection. Help us to acknowledge resurrection and everlasting life. Lord, hear us.

All: Lord, graciously hear us.

Leader:

In a moment of silence let us pray for each other and for all those
we love in the silence of our hearts.

When you lose someone you love,
your life becomes strange,
the ground beneath you becomes fragile,
your thoughts make your eyes unsure;
and some dead echo drags your voice down
where words have no confidence.
Your heart has grown heavy with loss;
and although this loss has wounded others too,
no-one knows what has been taken from you
when the silence of absence deepens.
Gradually, you will learn acquaintance
with the invisible form of your departed;
and when the work of grief is done,
the wounds of loss will heal
and you will have learned
to wean your eyes
from the gap in the air
and be able to enter the hearth
in your soul where your loved one
has awaited your return
all the time.

John O'Donohue

From Benedictus by John O'Donohue, published by Bantam Press.
Reproduced by permission of the Random House Group Ltd © 2007.

Leader:

Let us stand now, join hands with those around us, and say the words Jesus himself asked us to say:

Our Father, who art in heaven, hallowed be thy name.

Thy kingdom come; thy will be done on earth as it is in heaven.

Give us this day our daily bread and forgive us our trespasses as we forgive those who trespass against us.

And lead us not into temptation but deliver us from evil. For thine is the kingdom, the power and the glory for ever and ever.

Amen.

The sign of peace

Leader:

We now take time to offer our support to those around us with a sign of love and peace simply by saying "Peace be with you" and by shaking hands or sharing a hug or a kiss.

[PEOPLE OFFER ONE ANOTHER THE SIGN OF PEACE]

Please sit.

Thank you for your presence here tonight; our community will continue to hold you in prayer.

Before we go our separate ways, please say hello to someone who may be here alone this evening and who would welcome a few words of friendship and support.

Light refreshments will be served and we would love you to stay for a short while.

Thank you again for being here this evening. If you are not a parishioner or if you've not been here for some time, please do feel free to join us [*Times of services*]. We will always try to warmly welcome you: not one of us more important than anyone else; each of us made in the image and likeness of God; trying to support one another; holding each other in prayer.

Please sit for final words and blessing.

All:
May the love of God
and the peace of the Lord Jesus Christ
bless and console each one of us and all who grieve
and gently wipe every tear from our eyes:
In the name of the Father, and of the Son,
and of the Holy Spirit.
Amen.

Leader:
The words of our final song "I Will Come to You in the Silence" by David Haas offer us all great comfort and hope.

All sing:
"I Will Come to You in the Silence",
by David Haas.

Further reading

Much of the information in this book is based on the work of Rainbows Bereavement Support GB. It supports children and young people grieving a significant and often devastating loss in their lives.

The charity offers bereavement training to adults working with children and young people. It delivers training for facilitators and coordinators of the structured, peer-support Rainbows programmes: www.rainbowsgb.org

When Somebody Dies (Rainbows Bereavement Support GB). A practical resource to support schools to revise or review their policy and procedures for when somebody dies in their community.

SunRise (Rainbows Bereavement Support GB). A structured bereavement programme for adults and children with additional needs.

Marian Carter, *Helping Children and Adolescents Think about Death, Dying and Bereavement* (London: Jessica Kingsley, 2016)

Atle Dyregrov, *Grief in Children: A Handbook for Adults* (London: Jessica Kingsley, 2008)

Janet Goodall, *Children and Grieving* (London: Scripture Union, 1995)

Elisabeth Kübler-Ross, *On Death and Dying* (New York: Scribner, 1997)

Suzy Yehl Marta, *Healing the Hurt, Restoring the Hope* (London: Rodale, 2004)

Bill Merrington, *Death, Funerals and Heaven* (Stowmarket: Kevin Mayhew, 2009)

Doris Stickney, *Water Bugs and Dragonflies* (London: Continuum, 2004)

Mary Paula Walsh, *Helping your Child through Bereavement* (Dublin: Veritas, 2000)